A PORTFOLIO OF
BATHROOM
IDEAS

CREATIVE
PUBLISHING
international

MINNETONKA, MINNESOTA

CONTENTS

Copyright © 1994
Creative Publishing, international
5900 Green Oak Drive
Minnetonka, Minnesota 55343
1-800-328-3895

CREATIVE
PUBLISHING
international

President/CEO: David D. Murphy
Vice President/Editorial: Patricia K. Jacobsen
Vice President/Retail Sales & Marketing: Richard M. Miller

Library of Congress
Cataloging-in-Publication Data

A Portfolio of Bathroom Ideas

p. cm

ISBN 0-86573-926-9 (softcover)
1. Bathrooms—Design and construction.
I. Cy DeCosse Incorporated.
NK2117.B33P67 1994
747'.7'8—dc20   93-41245
Author: Home How-To Institute™
Creative Director: William B. Jones
Project Director: Paul Currie
Art Director: Lara Wyckoff
Project Manager: Kristen Olson
Writer: Stacy Sheagley
Copy Editor: Janice Cauley
Production Staff: Lara Wyckoff,
  Julie Sutphen
Vice President of Development
  Planning & Production: Jim Bindas
Production Manager: Amelia Merz

Printed on American paper by :
R. R. Donnelley & Sons Co.

10 9 8 7 6 5

WHAT MAKES A GREAT BATHROOM?

A great bathroom enables you to take care of your needs in a comfortable, attractive and convenient setting. Whether you are showering or shaving, a great bathroom lets you do so in a relaxed and pleasant fashion. It is a place you can retreat to in privacy, spending uninterrupted time tending to your needs. It reflects your individual sense of style by displaying your love of particular colors, your favorite textures and patterns. To help you plan your perfect bathroom, we have gathered over 150 color photographs of bathroom designs and styles and compiled them in *A Portfolio of Bathroom Ideas*.

This book will set you well on your way to creating a bathroom specifically suited to your taste and needs. First we cover the essentials of planning a great bathroom, such as determining what your needs are compared to your budget and learning how to recognize your own unique style. We then present the design elements for creating a wonderful bathroom: space (large and small), color (bright and dark), lighting (natural and artificial), and materials (marble, ceramic and wood). We show bathroom highlights that cover your choice of interesting appliances, unique fixtures and vanities. Then we elaborate on bathroom themes covering styles from country and romantic to garden and contemporary. Finally, we present pictures of distinctive bathrooms, where we show you unique ways to plan a bathroom theme and how to add to existing features. Whether you are starting from scratch or planning to remodel an existing bath, this book will help you plan a room that will not only meet your needs but will be a place of comfort, pleasure and even inspiration.

Photo courtesy of Kohler Co.

Photo courtesy of American Olean Tile Company

PLANNING

Assessing Your Needs

When considering bathroom decorating, whether you are thinking of completely remodeling or simply a face-lift, your first step is to determine your needs. Needs have to do with the people your bath will be servicing: how many of them there are and their ages, as well as how often they will be using it.

Are there just two of you, or do you have a large family? Maybe your home includes two working adults, both needing to get off to an early start each morning. Or perhaps your schedules allow you to make use of the same bath at different times during the day. What about children? Infants and young children have needs that are very

different from those of the growing teenager. Is there an elderly person living with you, or one who visits often? Special features that make bathrooms convenient and safe for individuals with specific needs and limitations can be incorporated.

Now is also the time to think of future needs, such as career development or planning a new family. Whether or not you will be staying in your home for years to come or want to move in a short time will also affect the type of decorating you'll be undertaking. Considering these aspects of your life will help you develop an image of your ideal bathroom.

Next you need to decide if you will be completely remodeling an existing bath, adding on an entirely new room, or simply redecorating a bathroom that is perfectly functional but in need of cosmetic changes.

Remodeling can be as simple as adding an extra washbasin or extensive enough to involve changing the plumbing in order to accommodate a whirlpool. Redesigning an existing bath generally includes replacing appliances and fixtures without changing the basic structure of the bath; more extensive work makes adding on a new room a more realistic option. Adding on also lets you have the fun of designing your dream bath, making the space exactly the size you want and giving you the chance to include amenities you might not otherwise be able to accommodate.

Another option to consider is the possibility of adding a half bath. These small rooms, including only a toilet and a sink, can alleviate the stress of inadequate bathroom space without involving a large amount of time, effort and money. An empty corner, an extra closet and even unused space under a stairway can be turned into a delightful and functional smaller bathroom.

Careful consideration of all these aspects, from the people in your life to what type of bathroom restructuring you want to undertake, is your first step toward a satisfying bathroom decorating experience.

PLANNING

Recognizing Your Style

Bathrooms come in as many styles as people do. Choosing a style that matches your personality is your second step after determining your needs.

What kind of atmosphere do you want this room to convey? Do you want it to be a friendly and welcoming room, or exotic, full of elaborate appliances and unusual odds and ends? This room can be a simple place with a basic color scheme and little ornamentation, or it can be full of fun, making use of bright, bold colors in interesting combinations and patterns. You might want to fill it with antiques, covering the walls with old-fashioned pictures and adding an armoire, or perhaps you would like to decorate all in white, adding just one other color as an accent.

As you consider your personal style and preferences, think of the rest of your house. What types of decorating schemes have you used in other rooms? Do you like them, or are there things about these rooms you would like to change?

Photos on this page courtesy of Kohler Co.

Looking at pictures in magazines or reading home improvement books is a great place to start. Notice which baths leap out at you. You can also visit model homes, noting the decorating schemes professionals have used.

Your style, once you have defined it, will be expressed in a variety of ways. You will be choosing colors and patterns, using materials such as wood or ceramic or stone, and deciding on sources of natural and artificial lighting. Each of

these areas is an avenue for personal expression. You might use them in imaginative ways or along more conservative lines. Perhaps you will pick a single theme to repeat throughout the room, or will want to take a more eclectic approach that combines many different techniques.

Whatever you choose, you want your bath to be a place you are comfortable in, a room that is as personal as your wardrobe and as familiar as a friend.

Planning

Determining Your Budget

Your final consideration, after assessing your needs and deciding upon your style, is your budget. How much money do you have to work with, and where is it coming from? You might wish to undertake a major renovation but only have enough money for a smaller remodeling job. Or perhaps you're willing to invest in an entirely new bath, whether that means building on a whole new room or restructuring an existing one. You will either have worked to save enough money for this new project, will be getting some type of loan or will be limiting yourself to a smaller decorating project that your current budget can handle.

While financing is usually available for home improvement, you should consider the value of your home as well as how long you plan to stay in it before making any final decisions. Adding a $6,000 bath to a home in a neighborhood of moderate incomes doesn't help the resale value;

however, a smaller redecorating job might be just the thing to make it marketable. If you plan to stay in your home, major changes make sense because you will be able to enjoy the added bath for years to come. New appliances are a large investment you might be able to skip if you currently have a newer bath with functioning appliances.

Sticking to adding accessories and changing the wallpaper lets you redecorate without great expense. However, if you are renovating an older home or adding on a bath, you will have to purchase appliances as well as additional features such as windows, mirrors and light fixtures. Whatever route you take, the budget you have to work with is a factor you must consider, along with your current needs and personal preferences. Thinking carefully about all these options before beginning will give you a good start toward creating a great bathroom.

SPACE

Size

Physical size is your number one consideration when determining bathroom decorating. How big or little is your bathroom going to be? Bathrooms come in various shapes and sizes, and whether you are creating an entirely new room or redecorating an existing bath will determine in part the options you will be working with.

For many people who are creating a bathroom from scratch, choosing a larger space allows them to develop a room that includes a variety of amenities and extra items a smaller room cannot provide. These can be everything from extra cupboards, drawers and counter space to additional appliances, such as a bidet or a shower stall separate from the tub.

Small baths are captivating, with their own versions of charm and style, and give you the chance to come up with creative uses of space. Interesting features are included in these smaller rooms: tiny windows and mirrors, unusual sinks, modest tables or shelves. In any case, remember that the size of your bath is only the beginning of your decorating experience.

The peaceful feeling of a private bathing area has been created in this room, although bedroom and bath occupy the same space. Set off from the rest of the room and placed at an angle, the tub occupies definite space that seems like a separate room. French doors leading outside lend a romantic air to the entire room.

Photo courtesy of Kohler Co.

Lots of unused floor space, combined with an all-white ceiling, gives this room a feeling of spaciousness. Appliances that encircle the room leave the middle area open for traffic flow or the addition of extra features, and add to its expansiveness.

Extra room is gained in this bathroom by tucking the toilet and bidet behind the shower area. An illusion of space can also be created by leaving the shower stall transparent and continuous with the rest of the bath.

Additional privacy is gained in this room by placing the toilet and bidet behind a half wall and down a step. This area, separate from the lavatory and full-length window, is hidden from view and allows the option of accommodating more than one individual at a time.

A popular feature in the larger bath is the installation of a shower separate from the tub. This room is set up to include a drying area outside the shower stall where towels, a robe and other clothing can remain dry, yet easily accessible. A glass block "window" between the tub and the shower visually connects this room's double bathing area.

The effect of two rooms instead of one has been created here by separating the bathing area from the rest of the bath. This feature is especially helpful when several people make use of the same bath, or it can be chosen simply to allow greater privacy.

Photos on this page courtesy of National Kitchen & Bath Association; project designed by Molly Korb, CKD, CBD

SPACE

Storage

Storage includes closets, drawers, shelves, cupboards and cupboards and cubbyholes that can hold accessories, linens and other items needed in the bathroom. Some baths are large enough to offer a variety of storage options. Others have little if any space for storage, making it necessary to utilize every available nook and cranny. Items used for storage can be selected to accentuate your design theme; you also may choose to be creative with objects not ordinarily associated with storage in the bathroom.

Shelves staggered next to the toilet allow a small reading area to be set up, while the extensive use of wall space aids in decorating this smaller bathroom.

This small vanity includes an assortment of cupboard and drawer spaces in interesting shapes and sizes. Lots of cupboards can be used, not only to store linens and personal accessories, but for any number of other household items.

With its many cubbyholes, this rustic cupboard provides a unique answer to the bath without closet space or one simply in need of extra storage. Rolling the towels rather than folding them makes creative use of available space.

COLOR

The color of your bathroom plays a close second to its size when making choices about bathroom decorating. You can feature colors that are bright and bold or of a quieter nature, perhaps the softer pastels. You might want to include several shades, using bright red to accent a softer gray, or a misty green and pastel pink against an off-white background.

Don't forget to consider the color schemes of other rooms in your home in order to maintain an overall sense of style. Remember that lighter colors, especially white, can make a room appear larger than it is and are especially helpful in smaller quarters; while darker colors have the effect of making a room look smaller, limiting their use in a small or medium-size bath, but making them an excellent choice for retaining intimacy in a larger room.

Choosing a color scheme also includes considering patterns. You can pick from many varieties of flowers, stripes, squares and other prints. You might choose to decorate with simple designs or along more intricate lines. Or come up with your own combination. Whatever your choice, color is an exciting medium to work with and offers you the chance to express your individuality, using various tones and interesting designs.

Photo courtesy of Color Tile, Inc.

Photo on opposite page courtesy of Armstrong World Industries, Inc.

Bright pink and aqua blue are used extensively in this bath, filling it with color. The floor, tub and sink make use of the same pattern, providing contrast to the quieter gray on the walls.

Using bright colors in a daring pattern on the floor, this room relies on simple stripes and a lighter color on the walls for softness and balance.

Color

An unusual color combination of sea green walls in contrast with a red floor and red trim around the mirror is used in this room. The stark white of the sinks and tub are reflected in the mirror and stand out in sharp relief against the heavier tones.

Fire-engine red, the sink, blinds and trim in this bathroom catch the eye while bold black tiles and a smaller black-and-white-pattern offer balance. Note the identical trim around the mirror and window; red blinds reflected in the mirror trick the eye into seeing it as another window. Or is the window really a mirror?

Photo courtesy of Grohe America

Photo courtesy of Color Tile, Inc.

This striking black lavatory with its pure white bowl is a bold addition to this room. Its strong visual presence creates a focal point that can be commanding on its own or used in combination with other interesting features.

White walls are set off sharply by the deep blue trim in this room. The sink and cabinets underneath become a focal point while blue-and-white towels complete this simple, yet striking, scheme.

Gray, pink and aqua blue combine to give this bathroom a quiet touch and extend an invitation to relax in this peaceful room at the end of a tiring day.

LIGHTING

Natural and Artificial

Lighting is an essential feature in every bathroom. We use both natural and artificial light daily in the various rooms throughout our homes. Windows let in natural light, connecting us to the sun and the world outside.

Natural light comes through windows. These can be just about any shape or size you choose, and can be set in various areas of the bath to create a specific atmosphere or tone. Paned windows are often placed next to or surrounding the tub, creating a bathing area separate from the rest of the room. Windows set above the sink provide extra light that helps with grooming. Uniquely shaped windows can become the room's focal point, apart from other features.

Windows can be customized, their interesting shapes serving a decorative as well as a practical purpose. Skylights provide depth as

Large windows not only let in lots of light, but also create a sense of spaciousness. Here the tub is set apart from the rest of the bath and surrounded with tall paned windows, giving the luxurious impression of an extra room and offering a vista of the world outdoors.

Lots of light comes into this room through these two large, angular windows. Because they are set at an angle and are continuous with the lines of the wall, they are an appealing decorating feature as well as a great source of natural light.

they let in light from unique and unexpected directions. Soft light sets a romantic tone, while bright lights illuminate dark corners.

Artificial light provides us with the ability to create light whenever we choose, making rooms functional at night. Beyond providing us with the ability to see, lighting can be used to create atmosphere and determine mood. Artificial light is available in different styles such as incandescent, which is very bright and an excellent choice around mirrors, or fluorescent, which is environmentally safe and less expensive.

Don't forget that wherever there is light, shadows appear, which provides intriguing decorating possibilities. Let your sources of natural and artificial light balance each other so that your room can be pleasantly lit any time of the day or night.

Photo courtesy of Armstrong World Industries, Inc.

Thick glass blocks cover nearly two full walls in this room, providing privacy as they let in light. A popular window choice that is also used as a room divider, glass blocks obscure images but allow ample light to shine through.

Three large, round skylights supply this spacious room with light from above, while glass blocks, mirrors and extra ceiling fixtures

provide an array of additional lighting possibilities that make each activity area functional and safe.

Photo courtesy of National Kitchen & Bath Association; project designed by Shelley Patterson, L. Jones

This room uses light from a variety of sources and directions. Windows, ceiling lights, fixtures above the mirror and the two lights directly over the bathtub provide a number of lighting options.

These two lighting examples, showing artificial versus natural light, display the differences in tone and mood between the two. Both types of light allow us to see, but artificial light can be used in softer tones to create a subtle effect, while bright natural light provides strong contrast with its shadows.

Photos on this page courtesy of Kohler Co.

In this room, glass blocks are again used for the window treatment. The large window area lets in light that, although diffused, is still bright, while it also provides privacy. The interesting shape and texture of glass block makes it an excellent decorating feature.

LIGHTING

Accoutrements

Lighting accoutrements are items such as mirrors and bathroom accents that combine with existing sources of light to provide additional illumination. They are used to enhance existing sources of light, but also serve as decorating features in themselves.

Beautifully arched and conveniently placed above the sink and counter area, this mirror reflects the rest of the bath in its smooth surface. Its unique shape gives an added dimension of elegance to this bath.

Bright light fills the eye in this all-white room, pouring in through the window and bouncing off the mirror and other reflective surfaces. Accents such as gold fixtures and yellow flowers provide warmth and depth, almost as if they were sources of light themselves.

Stained glass can be used for a unique lighting option, adding interesting color and pattern to the room. These ornate windows are decorated with bright flowers and intertwining vines. Available in a variety of designs, stained glass can also be made to order, letting you choose your own colors and patterns.

Colorful light spills into this room through two stained-glass windows made up of simple rectangles. Brilliant reds, yellows and blues spread over the floor, reflecting off the wall and the white appliances and filling the room with their warm hues.

MATERIALS

The materials you choose for your bath will be used to cover not only the walls and floor, but your appliances as well. You have the option of using a variety of materials, such as combining wooden cabinets and floors with ceramic tiles and porcelain appliances. Many other options are available, however, like stone, plastic laminates and vinyl flooring; your choice of material will help determine the atmosphere of the room and convey your bathroom theme.

Marble Bathrooms

Many varieties of stone and brick are available and are an interesting addition to the bath because of their various colors and textures. They can be used on the floor or the walls, and in combination with other materials, such as tile or wood. Marble, popular for its beautiful veined appearance and smooth surface, is an expensive material that is often used to convey an aura of wealth and splendor.

Marble, however, is easily stained and rather fragile. Synthetic marble that is practical, easier to install and less expensive is available.

This tub, encased in marble, includes such extras as additional space at one end, which can be used for seating or for conveniently storing accessories. A long marble shelf built flush against the wall also provides room for extra storage.

Here the entire bath has been covered with marble, including the walls, floor and bathing area. Surrounding the room with this one element conveys an image of elegance and richness.

Seen from the inside of this luxurious shower, marble walls enclose the stall with smooth stone, while a marble bench allows you to sit while showering. The same colored marble can be seen covering the rest of the bath as well.

Photo courtesy of National Kitchen & Bath Association; project designed by Stephanie Gisoldi

A deep green marble console sink is set up with bright brass fixtures, adding flair to its already rich surface. This combination fills the room with warmth and grandeur.

In this room, two distinct marble patterns complement each other. Dark marble contrasts with a lighter tan stone, providing a fitting background for this room's other distinctive features.

MATERIALS

Ceramic Tile

Ceramic tile is the most commonly chosen bathroom material, because it is easy to clean, water-resistant and long lasting. Available in a variety of colors and patterns, ceramic tile offers all sorts of decorating possibilities. You can combine patterns or use different colors for contrast. Best of all, ceramic is easy to maintain, a plus when it comes to cleaning up.

Simple blue tiles are used throughout this room, providing just one pattern and color. This effect is achieved by covering the porcelain tub and vanity with these tiles as well as the ceiling, walls and floor. Along with the appliances, a few well-placed flowers offset the heavy blue, adding diversion with a lighter color and an entirely different texture.

Tile in one color is used on the floor of this room, while another color, in a different style and size, has been placed on the wall. The contrast of both color and pattern adds excitement to the room.

Several styles of tile are used in this bath. Large white squares outlined in black cover the floor, while smaller pink tiles trimmed with accent tiles of black and blue are set around the tub. Finally, mosaics made up of all these tiles have been arranged on the wall above, adding a unique visual element.

Again we see a variety of tiles in complementary patterns and sizes working together to create an interesting room. Large and small diamonds, black against white, are used with tiny white and black squares, each complementing the other to create a stunning overall effect.

Photos courtesy of American Olean Tile Company

An arresting combination of black and gray tiles gives this bathing area a pristine atmosphere. Contrast can be provided with accessories; in this case, red and black towels on the wall and a dark green plant set next to the tub.

Blue and white tiles make up this room, again in various patterns. Here the small blue squares are used exclusively as trim, while diamonds cover the floor and larger squares highlight the expanse of counter space.

MATERIALS

Wood

Wood is a popular choice for bathroom cabinetry but can also be used for appliances, walls, ceilings and floors. It is durable and, if properly treated, stain-resistant; it also adds warmth to a room often outfitted with materials of a colder nature. There are a number of synthetic woods available, including oak, glued planks and butcher block, that are also durable and often just as pleasing to the eye as natural wood.

In this bath, oak cabinets in a variety of shapes and sizes are combined with a vanity base in the same pattern. A hardwood floor and wooden siding and trim extend the decor of this warm and friendly room.

Wooden cabinets are easy to install and come in a variety of styles. This cabinet features extra shelf space above and below the cupboard itself, providing additional storage.

This exquisite vanity is an example of wood used to create an object of great beauty. Delicately carved, the surface is highly polished to emphasize the wood's natural grain. The mirror on the wall above repeats the vanity's pattern and combines with it for a striking and elegant effect.

HIGHLIGHTS

Appliances

One easy way to highlight your bathroom is through your choice of appliances and fixtures. Available in a range of styles from classic to modern, these items allow you to fine-tune your bath, complementing your choice of material and color and elaborating on your basic bathroom theme. Highlights include basic appliances, such as the toilet, washbasin and tub, as well as extras like towel racks and soap dishes. Light fixtures are also a great way to add style to your bath.

Highlights other than appliances can be chosen for their flexibility as well as functionality. They are easily changed without much expense, letting you turn a room once meant for a child into one more suitable for a preteen. It doesn't take many of these items to promote style or convey a theme. Notice how various highlights make a statement about each of these rooms.

Demonstrating old-fashioned appliances combined with up-to-date style, this tub provides the best of both worlds. Smooth white porcelain rests on a dark oval base, while brass fixtures for both the tub and sink bring the two elements together. Handrails on either end of the tub add function with an extra touch of elegance.

This delicately curved sink is lovely enough to become this bathroom's focal point. Taking up little space, it would make a great addition to a smaller bath, providing an example of lots of style in a small package.

Toilet and matching pedestal sink are made of textured tile, adding an unusual visual and textural element to this bath.

Photos on these two pages courtesy of Kohler Co.

The appliances in this room glow from the light coming in from the windows above the yellow walls. The sink is trimmed with gold, as are the various fixtures on the appliances and the walls, adding to the room's unique coloring.

Fixtures come in a variety of styles and materials, and cover everything from faucets and door handles to cup holders and light covers.

Whether you choose ceramic knobs, sleek chrome faucets or bright brass handrails, these additions give depth to the design of your bath.

This unique shower enclosure offers aesthetic appeal in a highly technical setting. Shower heads, hand sprays, body sprays and other components allow a variety of showering options, from a fine mist to a soothing massage.

Designed along Victorian lines, this room contains an old-fashioned toilet with a wooden seat and wooden water tank set up high along the wall. A heavy porcelain pedestal sink repeats the design of the porcelain toilet. Brass fixtures are another fine feature in this handsome bath.

In this room a wall-mount lavatory and cistern are a unique addition to the bath. They offer an appliance option reminiscent of an earlier and more elegant era.

HIGHLIGHTS

Vanities

Vanities come in a variety of shapes, colors and styles and can be used to complement or elaborate upon your bathroom theme. They can be modern, mirrored and freestanding, or Queen Anne style with lots of cabinet space.

Vanities provide the perfect place to take care of your personal needs in peace. Consider introducing one in your bath and making it your own special place to prepare for the upcoming day or unwind before going to bed at night.

This vanity is set up with all the items necessary for personal care: a lamp for direct light, an oval mirror hung directly above the sink, natural light from the window, lots of cupboards and drawers beneath and, best of all, plenty of counter space.

Featuring a comfortable chair set next to the vanity, this lovely powder room is ready for its occupant to settle in for a quiet hour of grooming. This room has been designed as a special place of retreat, making it perfect to come to at the end of a hectic day.

Bathrooms with vanities that connect to the bedroom offer easy access for taking care of personal needs. This vanity provides plenty of counter space, allowing room for spreading out toiletries. Its curves duplicate those of the tub, making it visually consistent with the rest of the room.

A PORTFOLIO

of Bathroom Ideas

Charming
COUNTRY-STYLE
Bathrooms

What gives a bathroom country style? Is it the claw-foot tub, the antique fixtures, the wooden panelling or the braided rug set in the middle of the floor?

All of these features, as well as many others, can be found in the country bath. These rooms have a rustic edge. They make use of items commonly considered old-fashioned; everything from wicker chairs to tall wooden cabinets once used as wardrobes.

Consider what it is about the following rooms that give them a country feel. You might want to think of ways you can add to this theme, letting your special touch bring to life this favorite decorating scheme.

This room is truly rugged, with its chinked log walls and old-fashioned tub. Accessories play an important part in maintaining the theme of this cabin bath: antlers above the sink and fishing tackle next to old work boots set beneath a wooden, straight-backed chair secure the country focus of this room.

White paneled walls, an old-fashioned tub, a lovely hardwood cabinet and comfortable chintz chair represent the obvious elements that give this room a country air. Sun pouring in from the window completes the picture in this well-appointed bath.

Country style can be evoked with just a few items, like this simple oval mirror in a thin gold frame and the two tiny lamps nestled on either side. Old-fashioned pictures in heavy wooden frames add to the motif.

All the features you might expect to find in a country bath can be seen in this room: tall wooden cabinets, old-fashioned fixtures above the sink and corresponding accessories, such as small framed pictures grouped together around a simple square mirror. There is even a straight-backed chair tucked under a small wooden vanity.

Exquisite

ROMANTIC

Bathrooms

Romantic rooms are places where imagination runs wild and decor leans toward the extraordinary. They make use of extravagant features, often with a sentimental touch. Their colors are usually soft and their edges rounded. Draperies float in the breeze. Romantic rooms can be ornate and richly ornamented or more simply endowed, adorned with a few well-chosen objects.

This room is a reminder of old-world elegance, with its pillars and statuettes, vines running along the window frame and brightly shining ribbons. A large pedestal sink commands center stage, while an exquisite cut-glass window displaying a simple Grecian figure adds a final fanciful touch.

This sink, made of vitreous china, is covered with whimsical rabbits in cobalt blue. Accents such as the various jars, dishes and ceramic tiles repeat the design, adding to the lightness of this one small section of the room.

This bathroom corner features a classical pedestal sink. Heavy draperies tied back with tasseled cord, an intricately crafted mirror and a myriad of ornate accessories work together to suggest extravagance, a common romantic characteristic.

Photos on this page courtesy of Kohler Co.

Dainty curves and fluted edges turn this pedestal sink into a work of art. A simple pattern, delicately applied, runs along its edges, adding to its lightness and fragile grace.

Photo courtesy of Armstrong World Industries, Inc.

Peonies and ivy cover the inside of this basin, running along ceramic tiles on the wall and repeated on the fixtures. The sink is set inside a curved wooden vanity of deep mahogany, while an ornate Oriental carpet, glimpsed beneath, completes the romantic effect.

Pretty pinks suffuse this room with warmth and delicate color. Original features include a large, curved iron plant holder and matching settee. Sunlight shines in on a comfortable window seat. Notice the towels tucked into open cupboards set directly into the wall, a creative use of space as well as an interesting decorative feature.

Lovely GARDEN-STYLE *Bathrooms*

Garden-style bathrooms use natural elements for their theme. Whether cut flowers are set around in vases or climbing vines decorate the appliances, the garden bath has a fresh flavor, reminding us of colorful meadows and newly mown fields.

These bathrooms use natural furnishings, dried flower arrangements, and flowered wallpaper as well as lots of plants in hanging baskets or large pots set on the floor. They are rooms that liven the senses, filling you with a feeling of the outdoors. This theme will always be a bathroom favorite.

Fish swim on a sea-green wall above the tub in this garden bath, while a tall, green plant hovers over them, looking like seaweed, and sunlight streams in through the window. Even the wrought-iron chair looks as if it were made from twigs and branches.

Tiny pink and blue flowers decorate the appliances in this bath, matching a real basket of flowers set to one side. The delicacy of the flowered appliances, combined with bright light from the window, resembles a well-trimmed English garden full of forget-me-nots.

Lush green plants surround this tub. The base of the tub and the pedestal sink are trimmed with flowers, as if they are sitting in the middle of a garden.

This room is filled with flowers, both natural and painted. A decorative flower design covers the appliances and ceramic tiles, while on the wall above the sink, a mirror reflects the scene. Finally, vases of fresh flowers are set on shelves above the sink and toilet, surrounding the room with freshness.

Photo courtesy of Kohler Co.

Here a sink and matching accessories, brightly painted with red and yellow tulips, suggest a garden in spring. They are a lighthearted addition to any bath.

One wicker chair and a simple round log, set against the wall to serve as a table, are elements that give this bath a carefree, natural touch. A tall green plant next to the tub and a flowered picture on the wall add to the outdoor flavor of this room.

Fabulous

CONTEMPORARY

Bathrooms

The contemporary bath contains up-to-date features in a modern setting. Following current trends, this type of bath is often technologically advanced, filled with state-of-the-art appliances and fashionable highlights. Design is often angular, or along more straightforward lines.

The beauty of this type of bath lies in its simplicity; however, this does not mean it lacks allure. The following rooms are filled with features that enhance their simpler styles.

This modern bath makes use of appliances built along simple lines that are geometrically shaped. The room is large, containing both a toilet and bidet, a tub and a separate shower stall. In the middle of the room stands the lavatory, complete with a huge mirror and lots of shelf and counter space. Various types of lighting are used, from "fluorescent" bulbs by the mirror to incandescent fixtures above the tub, while from above, a large, square skylight spreads light and shadow across the walls and floor, creating patterns that repeat the room's simple lines.

Photo courtesy of Kohler Co.

Tiled steps lead up to a large, angular tub, this room's main feature. Placed under a glass block wall, the tub is filled with unobstructed sunlight. This window eliminates the need for draperies or other window coverings. A comfortable striped couch occupies one wall of the room, while accents such as candles, a decorative plate and an abstract painting are also used. Notice the angular mirror above the sink, also a contemporary feature.

This room makes use of rounded edges and gentle curves, an earlier style that has again become popular. The shell-shaped light fixture above the counter is especially interesting. An arched window set above the tub and across from the vanity is reflected in the mirror's glass.

Textured pearl gray walls and bright white appliances are the arresting features in this modern room. The canopy beneath the sink serves as decorative cover for the plumbing.

The details in this room are elaborate. The sink is lined with gold, and gold hardware is used throughout the room. Notice the geometric design at the base of the bidet. Even the legs of the lavatory are distinctively shaped, with intricate knobs capping them off at the top.

Light from the window bounces off this modest washbasin and is reflected back onto the tiny tiles on the wall. The design of the sink is uncomplicated, in keeping with contemporary styles, which prize the plain and unadorned.

DISTINCTIVE

Bathrooms

Bathrooms that are distinctive include elements that go beyond what is usually expected in the bath. They are unique, perhaps because their purpose is unusual or because they are filled with extraordinary items.

These kinds of baths lift us beyond our expectations to delightful, even exhilarating heights. They stretch the imagination, making us think of exciting possibilities we might not otherwise have considered. Set your imagination free as you explore the unusual elements of these remarkable rooms.

Family

Bathrooms that are used by an entire family, no matter how many people this includes, should be designed to meet a variety of needs. Consider the following if you are designing this type of bath: Is there enough room? Is it easy to care for, and does it provide privacy? Can it accommodate both genders? Will children be using it? What about company?

The family bath, although needing to be efficient, does not have to be limited by this need. Have fun when designing this type of room. Be creative, considering the personalities of those who will be using it. Ask for their ideas. The family bath will see lots of action; make it friendly as well as practical.

Photos courtesy of National Kitchen & Bath Association; project designed by Shelley Patterson, L. Jones

Suited to meet the needs of both sexes, this room provides plenty of space without a loss of privacy. The tub is hidden behind a curved wall of glass block, while linen is stored in a separate section that doubles as a dressing area. There is even enough room for the morning cup of coffee!

Two sinks, two mirrors, a toilet, a bidet and the traditional enclosed tub-and-shower combination make this bright blue bathroom a family favorite. Completely tiled and easy to clean, it sets the standard for any family bath.

Featuring bright colors and bold patterns, this child's bathroom has been built with appliances that are low to the ground and easy to reach. The shower, set up with a detachable nozzle, makes washing up painless and quick.

Sporting two sinks, lots of cupboards, shelves and drawers, a large tub and, most important of all, plenty of floor space, this bathroom is perfect for a family of any size. An added plus is the unlimited availability of light; fixtures have been placed in such a way that light can be shed on all the main areas of activity.

DISTINCTIVE BATHROOMS
Workout

Many people have added exercise to their daily routine and are faced with the problem of storing equipment that is utilized every day, but only for limited periods of time. One solution is letting the bathroom double as a private workout facility.

Adding exercise equipment to the bath is an easy way to include this important activity to your routine and offers the added convenience of a ready shower when the workout is through. It also lets you store your workout equipment in a room where it will be out of the way when not in use.

Both a rowing machine and an exercise bike fit into this large bathroom area. One of them was placed in the hall outside the main room to save on space, a unique storage idea.

This bath contains enough room for stretching out before starting the workout. The exercise bike has been set in a corner, where it occupies little room and does not detract from the main bathing area.

Photo courtesy of Andersen Windows, Inc.

Photo courtesy of Congoleum Corporation

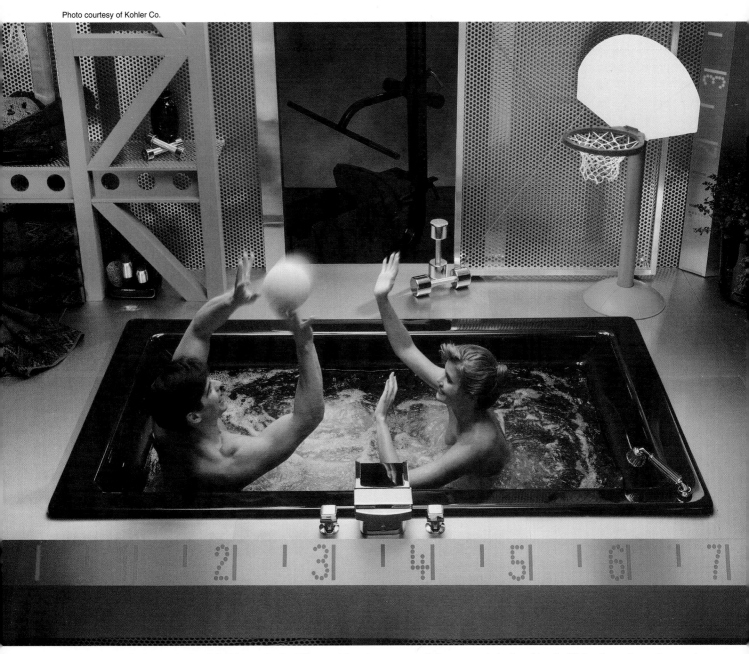

In this creative bath, the whirlpool doubles as a basketball court. There is room enough for two people in the tub, and additional exercise equipment sits outside the bathing area, which has been designed to look like a playing field.

DISTINCTIVE BATHROOMS
Deluxe

Rich in style and comfort, the following rooms contain everything from fireplaces and overstuffed armchairs to television sets. Deluxe bathrooms have lavish features that make them luxurious. Filled with an abundance suggestive of great wealth, some contain duplicate matching appliances, while others provide intricate decorations or a variety of comfortable amenities.

Deluxe baths contain original designs in elaborate settings. Enjoy the following rooms; even if you do not aspire to this type of setting for your own bath, you can still take pleasure in their splendor and find inspiration in their elaborate decor.

Rich in style and comfort, this room contains everything from a fireplace, comfortable chairs and softly lit lamps to a recessed bathing area with a shower stall on one side and a separate room for the toilet on the other. These are set off from the main room by curtained panels in a delicate floral print while the vanity resides in the middle of the room. A sink sits on one side, counter space is available on the other and a mirror has been hung in the middle. This is truly a magnificent room.

Photo courtesy of Armstrong World Industries, Inc.

The pleasures of television have been added to this bath with not one, but two, T.V.'s set in the wall above a built-in shelf, a convenient way to catch up on the morning news on different channels! Again we see rolled towels set into an open cupboard area. A long shelf has been built next to the sink, where several odds and ends are conveniently stored.

Photo courtesy of Kohler Co.

Here a triangular shower stall, occupying one corner of the bath, takes up little room but is a perfect place for two to shower in comfort. This roomy stall is designed with two shower heads and two sets of faucets, ending the debate over how hot or cold the shower should be.

Perfect for the powder room, this Queen Anne style double-basin vanity is designed for convenience as well as beauty. Built of hardwood with a china basin, polished brass faucets and lots of storage space, it is set off with the addition of matching framed mirrors and twin wall-mounted lamps.

A washbasin lined with strips of gold brightens this sink area, while matching fixtures add an extra burst of luxury.

Spaciousness dominates this room, allowing the functional features to blend into the background. The room includes a black tub and black double washbasins, an arched window set high above the sink with matching arched beams in the middle of the room, padded seats, lots of cupboards and plenty of windows covered with vertical blinds. Small, square rust-colored tiles cover the floor and lead up to the tub, filling the room with their warm, polished glow.

DISTINCTIVE BATHROOMS
Exotic

Exotic bathrooms are filled with sensational and elaborate props. They invite us to indulge in a world of make-believe where we can inhabit our dreams, even if only for a time.

Making use of unusual appliances, original combinations and novel structures, they suggest a place where fantasy becomes reality and where the unexpected is customary.

As with the deluxe bathroom, while you might never create a bath as elaborate as these, you can still appreciate their originality and perhaps be inspired to include an exotic element in your own bath.

First to grab the eye in this unique bath is a thin, freestanding black wall set in the middle of the room, serving as both a room divider and a background for the sink and mirror. Behind it sit the toilet and bidet; in front are an overstuffed armchair and footstool. Steps lead up to the ceramic tub, while the impression of an old-world garden is evoked by stone planters filled with climbing vines.

Photo courtesy of Kohler Co.

Serene blue and simple white on the walls and floor are a fitting background to this bath, with its carved pillars and dazzling white lavatory molded from a single ceramic piece. Tall palms wave in the background behind the curved tub, while natural light is diffused throughout the room.

An Oriental pattern in sculpted green waves drapes across this china basin, while black and gold accents add extra elegance.

This exotic wooden vanity, reminiscent of Far Eastern furnishings, adds an unusual touch to this bath. Its features include a black octagonal basin and plenty of drawer and counter space. A zebra skin, serving as a rug, adds additional foreign flair to the room.

Photos on this page courtesy of Kohler Co.

In an unusual turn of events, two wrought-iron chairs, a settee with golden tassels and a gilt-framed mirror set the tone for this oval room, while the large pedestal sink and claw-foot tub in the background serve as accompaniments. Blue pin-striped wallpaper and a powder blue curtain knotted and draped across the room add flair and individuality.

Flowers fill this sink, merging together at the bottom as if from a single plant. The basin is set in a green marble console, while the handles are trimmed with the same flower design and set on either side of an antique polished-brass faucet.

Console tables provide counter space without taking up room. This elaborate design, set directly into the wall, is made of marble with antique faucets of polished brass and elaborately carved wrought-iron legs.

93

DISTINCTIVE BATHROOMS
Special Needs

The tub in this room allows easy access with its hinged door and built-in handrail. The door to the tub seals tight inside, preventing the possibility of leakage. Just walk in, close the door and turn on the water! The toilet is wheelchair-accessible, and the wide sink, jutting out past the counter's edge, is within easy reach from a sitting position.

Recently bathrooms designed with appliances and fixtures that meet the needs of those who are physically challenged have become widely available. Not simply utilitarian, these rooms are attractive and inviting places featuring customized appliances that are pleasant to look at while providing independence for those with special needs.

Providing such features as an adjustable sink able to accommodate a wheelchair and a comfortable folding seat in the shower area, this room has handrails placed next to the toilet for added support and easy-to-use faucets and fixtures. Wood panelling and a wood-framed mirror add a rustic element to this pleasant, yet functional, room.

LIST OF CONTRIBUTORS

We'd like to thank the following companies for providing the photographs used in this book:

American Olean Tile Company
1000 Cannon Avenue
Dept. BD
Lansdale, PA 19446-0271
215-393-2237

American Standard
1 Centennial Plaza
Piscataway, NJ 08855
For the free guide book, We Want You to Love Your
Bathroom, call 1-800-524-9797

Andersen Windows, Inc.
P.O. Box 3900
Peoria, IL 61614
1-800-426-4261

Armstrong World Industries, Inc.

Bates & Bates
3699 Industry Ave.
Lakewood, CA 90712
1-800-726-7680

Color Tile, Inc.
515 Houston St.
Fort Worth, TX 76102
1-800-688-8063
Over 800 Color Tile and Carpet locations coast to
coast. Check the white pages of your telephone
directory for the one nearest you.

Congoleum Corporation
3705 Quakerbridge Rd.
Mercerville, NJ 08619
1-800-934-3567

Grohe America
241 Covington Drive
Bloomingdale, IL 60108
708-582-7711

Kohler Co.
Kohler, WI 53044
1-800-4-KOHLER

Kraftmaid Cabinetry, Inc.
Suite 239 The Hanna Building
1422 Euclid Ave.
Cleveland, OH 44115
1-800-654-3008

National Kitchen & Bath Association
687 Willow Grove St.
Hackettstown, NJ 07840
1-800-FOR-NKBA

Porcher Ltd.
3618 E. LaSalle St.
Phoenix, AZ 85040
1-800-338-1756

Stained Glass Overlay of St. Paul/Minneapolis
Suite 9
2660 Cleveland Ave. N.
Roseville, MN 55113
612-628-0308

Gallop Studios
Suite 103
2500 Broadway St. N.E.
Minneapolis, MN 55343
612-379-8040